CARCASSI
MELODIC AND PROGRESSIVE ETUDES, Op. 60

WITH FINGERINGS BY AARON SHEARER
AND PERFORMANCE NOTES BY THOMAS KIKTA, KAMI ROWAN, AND RICARDO COBO

AN ALFRED CLASSICAL GUITAR MASTERWORK EDITION

Cover art:
L' Allegro (Italian Sunset) (1845)
by Thomas Cole
(American, 1801-1848)
Oil on canvas, 81.6 cm x 121.76 cm
Los Angeles County Museum of Art,
Los Angeles, California, USA
Wikimedia.org

Image of Aaron Shearer courtesy of
the Aaron Shearer Foundation

Sound recording and post production engineer:
Thomas Kikta

Alfred Music
P.O. Box 10003
Van Nuys, CA 91410-0003
alfred.com

Copyright © MMXVI by
The Aaron Shearer Foundation
All rights reserved. Printed in USA.

Produced by Alfred Music

ISBN-10: 1-4706-1524-X
ISBN-13: 978-1-4706-1524-6

MATTEO CARCASSI

Contents

Stream or download the audio content for this book.
To access online audio, visit: **www.alfred.com/redeem**
Enter the following code: **00-42723_882288**

Melodic and Progressive Etudes, Op. 60
With fingerings by Aaron Shearer
and performance notes by Thomas Kikta, Kami Rowan, and Ricardo Cobo

Foreword

Perhaps no other classical guitar etudes have been upheld as the basic training ground for technique as much as Matteo Carcassi's Op. 60, *25 Etude Mélodiques*. These 25 studies offer a foundation for developing the basic to advanced left- and right-hand techniques we find applied throughout our literature. Carcassi was able to embed these useful techniques in a collection of lovely musical vignettes that are enjoyable both to the player and the listener.

So why publish another edition of these etudes when, because of copyright expiration, they are easily available for free? We believe we can offer an insightful pedagogical perspective based on the intersections of our knowledge of the works of this amazing composer, Carcassi, and the teachings of one of the best-known guitar pedagogues, Aaron Shearer. This edition is based on Aaron Shearer's personal markings and his approach to performing Carcassi's Op. 60, *25 Etude Mélodiques*.

Our perspectives are rooted in our work with Aaron Shearer in our undergraduate studies and beyond. While our life and teaching experiences have informed us in ways different from our work with Shearer, we find his views very insightful and valuable. We may not have covered every single technical issue or point in each of Carcassi's etudes, but we attempted to bring to light things unique to Shearer's way of thinking. We hope you will find this book sheds new light on, and adds to your appreciation of, these wonderful etudes—especially with the addition and online availability of an audio recording by Ricardo Cobo. Although Mr. Cobo exercised some artistic license in his performances, they are still an excellent resource when learning these important etudes with this book.

You may come across terms or concepts in the front section of the book that are unfamiliar. We have added footnotes in many places, offering references to specific Aaron Shearer books where they are explained. If you are not learning the pieces in order, and thus not reading the front matter in order, keep in mind that an unfamiliar term may be footnoted earlier.

Please visit our Carcassi Supplement at www.aaronshearerfoundation.org for additional insights, edits, and supplemental discussions that go beyond the scope of this book.

–Thomas Kikta, Kami Rowan, and Ricardo Cobo

Etude No. 1

pg. 20

Purpose

At first glance, the focus of "Etude No. 1" appears to be the alternation of *i* and *m*[1] in a scalar context. With some creative right-hand adjustments, however, Aaron Shearer not only emphasizes alternation but also the application of *sympathetic motion*[2] in right-hand scale fingerings. By using *a*, *m*, and *i* on the first three treble notes in measure 1, a sympathetic arpeggio fingering is introduced as a substitute for alternation. The remainder of the scale should be played with *i* and *m* alternation. Sympathetic motion occurs again in measure 21, but this time with an *i–m–a* arpeggio pattern. Finally, measures 29–35 contain repeated *p–i–m–a* arpeggios,[3] again bringing sympathetic motion to the forefront in this piece.

The beauty of sympathetic motion is the timing and organization of the hand in a sequential movement that supports collective flexion or extension of the fingers. The fingers work as a team, promoting relaxed finger motion and assisting in grouping notes together, especially in quick passages. Another advantage of using the *a* finger to initiate scales in this etude is that it minimizes awkward right-hand *string crossings*[4] that tend to happen with strict *i–m* alternation. Additionally, as *p* plays a bass note, the *a* finger is closer to the 1st string than *i* or *m*, which means the player can take advantage of the spacing of the fingers in relation to the string groupings.

Technical Issues

Isolating the opening measure a few times will make it evident that proper form in right-hand string crossing is very important. Practicing in front of a mirror will help to make sure the wrist is not deviated and the shoulder/arm joint is not changing position as the right arm and hand transition across strings. If string crossing is done correctly—using the elbow—the hand will make a slight diagonal arc as it crosses the strings. Be aware of the string-crossing challenges in measures 11, 15, 20, and 22. Realistically, *cross fingerings*[5] in the right hand cannot be completely eliminated, but they should be minimized. When these do occur (e.g., the end of measure 3 into 4), pay special attention to the relationship between the string crossing and the placement of the next finger. This might feel awkward at first, but it is a reality that guitarists must deal with.

---

1   *The Shearer Method*, Book 1, pg. 97 introduces the alternation of *i* and *m*.
2   *The Shearer Method*, Book 1, pg. 63 introduces sympathetic motion.
3   *The Shearer Method*, Book 1, pg. 90 introduces the *p–i–m–a* arpeggio.
4   *The Shearer Method*, Book 1, pg. 151 includes a definition and demonstration of string crossing.
5   *The Shearer Method*, Book 1, pg. 157 includes a definition and example of cross fingering.

Aaron Shearer's concept of *Aim-Directed Movement* (ADM) is a very powerful way to understand the movement of your hands on the guitar as you progress through a piece. In short, ADM means knowing where, when, what, and how to move before actually moving. The foundation of ADM is created through the process of *pre-reading*, which provides an opportunity to work away from the guitar by taking a few measures at a time, saying notes or solfeggio syllables aloud, and seeing in the "mind's eye" where these notes lay on the instrument. After clarifying the segment with pre-reading, the player would then play it on the guitar, continuing to say aloud the notes or solfeggio syllables. Shearer called this "play and say."[6] The goal is to work slowly to minimize confusion and error, while raising cognitive awareness and gaining control. These activities will clarify the understanding of the movement of the hands and will create clear aims with which you will ultimately direct your movements.

ADM should always be applied in your practice but will especially help develop accuracy while shifting in measures 29–33. Applying ADM also assists in developing an understanding of what is required to achieve maximum mechanical advantage.

In measure 29, a four-string left-hand barre[7] at the 3rd fret is indicated with a small subscript 4 next to the BIII. It is important to barre only the necessary amount of strings. This type of notation will be employed throughout this edition.

The Shearer Perspective

In a lesson focusing on "Etude No. 1" with Aaron Shearer, one could expect to focus on string crossing and sympathetic motion. With string crossing, Shearer would specifically look for any movement not initiating from the elbow and require that the right hand maintain the same position across all the strings. He would also make sure that sympathetic motion, such as in the *p–i–m–a* arpeggios, was truly sympathetic and not slipping into individual, or independent, finger motions. Finally, to add a technical challenge, Shearer would suggest this etude be practiced with the more-difficult *m–a* alternation as an alternative to *i–m*. This approach would strengthen your *m* and *a* alternation playing, which is often neglected, while promoting fluency in the right hand.

Performance Notes

Fluency should be a priority when performing "Etude No. 1." Start with *i–m* alternation (rather than the *m–a* alternation mentioned above for study purposes), so the etude can move quickly. Notice that the composer

indicates staccato in measure 1. Keep the mood of this study light and rhythmically tight. Ensuring the eighths and quarters in the bass remain short will give "Etude No. 1" a crisp character. Be sure to emphasize the conversation, or dialogue, between the two voices in measures 9–20. Give attention to the antecedent-consequent phrases as they are presented in treble–bass dialogue. Finally, dynamically emphasize the phrasing of the bass line in measures 29–35.

Etude No. 2

pg. 22

Purpose

While we do not know Carcassi's intentions for right-hand fingering in this piece, the purpose of this etude historically has been the application of *m–a* and/or *i–m* alternation following the *p–i–m–a* arpeggio. Striving to make the *m–a* alternation sound as strong and fluent as the *i–m* alternation is a great goal for this study. Though *m–a* alternation may not be as prevalent as *i–m* in scale work, it is imperative to practice *m–a* and gain equal fluency and freedom in both alternation combinations.

Shearer's alternate right-hand fingerings (illustrated in the music) create a very interesting 12-note pattern, where *i* and *a* alternate against *m*. If there is a deficiency in the *m–a* alternation, it will be clearly felt or heard when it is directly juxtaposed against the *i–m* alternation. Practice slowly to emphasize evenness of sound in all fingers. With Shearer's alternate fingerings, "Etude No. 2" is put into 16th-note triplets. Thus, as illustrated in the music, the descending bass line in measure 16 will also change.

Technical Issues

"Etude No. 2" introduces many commonly used triads[8] and their inversions on the treble strings of the guitar. Learning to identify the names and shapes of these triads is a good theoretical study goal and an effective tool in the memorization process.

Shifting from triad to triad frequently presents the opportunity to employ a *guide shift, guide finger,* or *glide finger.*[9] For example, in measure 1, the 2nd finger can remain on the 3rd string while shifting to the next chord. This occurs often, so it is important to identify all the guide fingers in this piece during pre-reading to assist in accurate shifting. Place individual left-hand fingers only as needed while shifting, as it is not necessary to shift with a block chord. This will allow for more-fluent shifting and transitioning between chords.

---

6   The text and videos in *The Shearer Method*, Book 1, pg. 9 introduces pre-reading and "play and say." Additional information and videos can be found in *The Shearer Method*, Book 2, pg. 7, and at the *Shearer Online Supplement* (www. aaronshearerfoundation.org).

7   *The Shearer Method*, Book 2, pg. 94, Classic Guitar Developments, introduces the barre.

8   *The Shearer Method*, Book 1, pg. 121 includes additional information on triads.

9   *The Shearer Method*, Book 1, pg. 77 defines the guide shift or glide finger shift

The diminished 7th chord on the first two beats of measure 5 might cause a player to raise their left-arm elbow upward and outward in an unnatural manner. Though it is important for the hand and arm to yield to the pull of the fingers, be careful not to raise your elbow excessively here, as doing so will also make the shift to the next chord more difficult.

Be sure to pay attention to changes in string groupings with the right hand. The majority of "Etude No. 2" is a 4–3–2–1 string grouping, but at measure 16, Carcassi transitions to a 6–4–2–1 grouping. Isolating transitions from one string group to another on open strings with the right hand can clarify the specific crossing spacing and string grouping.

The Shearer Perspective

Aaron Shearer liked to explore alternate right-hand patterns in this Carcassi etude. These additional right-hand groupings allow students to get more right-hand practice out of a single piece of music. Shearer's favorite alternate right-hand arpeggio for "Etude No. 2" was this arpeggio containing two six-note groupings: *p–m–i–a–m–a* and *i–m–i–a–m–a*, which can be played with the same left-hand chords. Shearer also explored placing the emphasis on different fingers by changing this into a three-note grouping: *p–m–i, a–m–a, i–m–i* or *p–m–i, a–m–a, a–m–a*. When using Shearer's alternate right-hand fingering, emphasis the *p* in *p–m–i* and the first *i* in *i–m–i* to create a longer musical line.

Another signature Shearer concept is to place a left-hand finger or barre earlier than needed to create an easier transition. For example, although there is no barre needed in measure 19, employing one prepares you for the upcoming barre in measure 20. This prevents the 1st finger from hopping into the barre position as it transitions from measure 19 to measure 20. In Shearer's studio, this *a–m* alternation etude was a precursor to more-complex alternation exercises like Heitor Villa-Lobos's "Etude No. 1."

Performance Notes

Using *i–m* alternation as opposed to *m–a* will ultimately enable more fluency and speed. In addition, employing dynamics in performance can add a great deal of intensity and contrast to the longer phrases of the 12-note pattern.

Etude No. 3

pg. 24

Purpose

The main focus of "Etude No. 3" is the execution of an *a–i–m* arpeggio[10] with a melodic emphasis on *a* while playing a counter melody with an emphasis on *p*. This creates a musical dialogue between the two lines that can be carried out through the entire piece.

Technical Issues

The key to the *a–i–m* arpeggio is maintaining *m* and *a* in sympathetic motion while an alternation occurs between *i* and *m*. The opening *p–i–m–a* arpeggio is fully sympathetic. However, when *a* sounds the melody on the 1st string, *i* should extend to create an alternation between *i* and *m–a*. This exchange occurs throughout the arpeggio. Keep *m* and *a* moving sympathetically, even at the end of the pattern during the *p–i–m* arpeggio.

Be sure to use the left-hand 2nd finger as a guide finger to D when transitioning from measure 1 to measure 2.

Measures 3–4, 7–8, and 15–16 provide opportunities to use a guide finger as in "Etude No. 2." Allow a guide finger to assist in each shift.

Measures 13–15 highlight the use of left-hand sequential placement, in which fingers arrive at the fret only as needed.

The Shearer Perspective

Shearer consistently recommended that students pre-read a score in order to resolve difficult passages before playing them on the guitar. Measure 16 is a good example: the distinct rhythmic variation in the duplet subdivision should be conducted with the right hand/arm while saying or singing the notes. This process will clarify the rhythm prior to reading and build accuracy and confidence while playing.

Shearer would also encourage the use of a mirror as a feedback mechanism to visually ensure proper right-hand form and correct sympathetic motion. Make sure the *m–a* movement is sympathetic while a clear alternation is occurring between *i* and *m*.

Performance Notes

"Etude No. 3" is a lovely melodic piece in a major key. Note that it is important to create a flow with the right-hand arpeggio while still maintaining a clear dialogue between the *a*-finger melody line and *p*-finger bass line.

---

10 *The Shearer Method*, Book 2, pg. 151 introduces the *a–i–m* arpeggio.

Etude No. 4

pg. 26

Purpose

"Etude No. 4" is a slur study that emphasizes triplet pull-offs on the 1st string and the use of ascending *p–i–m–a* sympathetic patterns. In addition, Shearer advocates the use of a *rest slur*.[11] When a rest slur is executed on an inner string, the slurring (pull-off) finger should come to rest on the higher adjacent string. Since all the slurs in "Etude No. 4" are on the 1st string, one should apply the same movement principle while pulling off the 1st string: the direction of the slur will be the same, parallel to the plane of the fretboard (or downward toward the floor).

Technical Issues

The B-note reference in measure 22 is a modification from the original score that makes the note pattern consistent with the rest of the piece. The editors of this edition believe this may have been a misprint in the first edition.

Guitarists tend to shorten the downbeat and rush the triplet slurs by hammering-on or pulling-off unevenly. Therefore, it is important to count and feel the first beat (downbeat) as a sextuplet, and the second beat as two triplets. Before playing, isolate the core movements in the triplet hammer-on/pull-off, so that they are as balanced as possible. One should strive to maintain a balanced and rhythmically even sound throughout.

Some of the bass notes in "Etude No. 4" should be muted or stopped with *p*. This muting should occur when there are open strings that ring over into a new or different harmony. Some examples of bass-note dampening in this etude are: the E bass from measure 5 for the downbeat of measure 6, the A bass in measure 6, the E bass from measure 7 for the downbeat of measure 8, the E bass from measure 13 for the downbeat of measure 14, and the A bass from measure 20 for the downbeat measure 21. Placing *p* on the overlapping bass should be done by touching the back of *p* exactly before the downbeat as part of the execution of *p* at the downbeat.

The Shearer Perspective

Shearer would make sure that the right-hand movement in this study was working correctly. In the opening *p–i–m–a* sequence, *a* alternates with *m* as it slurs, then *a* and *m* alternate twice with each other before closing the pattern with a final *a–m* sympathetic motion. In a lesson, Shearer would make sure the student could feel the difference between *a* and *m* moving sympathetically and the *a–m* alternation.

Performance Notes

When practicing "Etude No. 4" for technical considerations, one should use the *m–a* alternation to develop skill with this less-familiar pattern. However, when transitioning to faster performance tempos, the use of an *i–m* alternation may prove to be more fluent.

Etude No. 5

pg. 28

Purpose

The primary purpose of "Etude No. 5" is to practice the execution of alternation between *p* and the fingers. This study is a nice precursor to "Etude No. 6," where *p* is utilized repeatedly without any finger alternation. Carcassi's "Etude No. 5" is a *Moderato* piece that illustrates a melodic bass line with contrapuntal movement built with alternating 3rds, 6ths, and 10ths. The descending and opposing voices will challenge the student to bring out important melodic lines. The first three measures of "Etude No. 5" are excellent examples of alternating top and bottom voices.

Technical Issues

This etude presents an opportunity for the player to evaluate the form and motion of the right-hand thumb, *p*. The motion of *p* should initiate from the wrist joint, be firm and strong, and follow through, bringing it to rest on the *i* tip joint.[12] Unlike an upstroke with a finger, *p* uses a downstroke, which produces a different and more-accented sound. In this study, *p* plays the downward-stemmed eighth notes, creating a slight accent on the implied melodic line.

In "Etude No. 5," students must determine which voices require definition and accent, thus challenging them to slightly accent and balance the lines with *p* and their fingers as necessary.

Once again, guide shifts are used throughout this etude. Maintaining the 2nd finger on the transition from C to B in measure 3 to 4 enhances security and clarity of left-hand shifting. Similar guide-finger shifts occur at measures 8–9 and 13–14. These shifts occur in numerous places throughout "Etude No. 5," so it could be helpful to highlight these spots while pre-reading.

An awkward fingering in the left hand occurs in the transition from measure 2 to 3. The C on the downbeat of measure 3 is played with the 2nd finger. This fingering is tricky since the 3rd finger has just played G on the 6th string. This happens again in the transition to the following measure, when the 2nd finger plays a B on the downbeat as finger 1 has just played an A on the 3rd

---

11 For more information on rest slurs, see *The Shearer Method*, Book 2, pg. 52 and the *Shearer Online Supplement*.

12 *The Shearer Method*, Book 1, pg. 5 outlines the proper use of *p*.

string. Allow the arm and hand to yield to the pull of the fingers by bringing the elbow in toward the torso to make these fingerings easier.

The Shearer Perspective

Measure 9–10 and 17–20 use a *p–i–m–a* arpeggio followed by a string crossing and *m–a* alternation. Shearer would check that *i*, *m*, and *a* are truly working sympathetically in the arpeggio. He would also make sure that all string crossings are initiated from the elbow, and finally, that *m* and *a* are executing a strict alternation.

Performance Notes

It is important to understand the melodic content in "Etude No. 5" through a thorough investigation of the contrapuntal nature of the piece. The application of legato within each line will assist in the delivery of the separate lines and allow more clarity for the listener.

Etude No. 6

pg. 30

Purpose

While "Etude No. 5" sets the stage for reviewing the habits of motion with *p*, "Etude No. 6" brings the application of *p* to the forefront. The opening eight measures present material that offers the right-hand thumb an opportunity to achieve a focused and consistent tone while playing as legato as possible. Working in front of a mirror while learning this etude can help ensure good habits of *p* motion.

Technical Issues

Measure 8 incorporates a "phantom guide" finger, where the 4th finger stays on the 1st string as the hand shifts to play F♯ and G with the 2nd finger. This provides a stable reference to guide the hand during the shift.

Measures 9–11 apply an *a–m–i–m* arpeggio form to a linear melodic line. The *a–m–i–m* arpeggio is one of the five right-hand patterns that does not utilize *p*.[13] This is a good movement form to isolate to ensure the sequence of the fingers is correct. The *a* and *m* fingers move sympathetically, followed by an alternation between *i* and *m*, as *m* and *a* extend. At the end of the arpeggio, another alternation occurs between *m* and *a*, while *m* extends with *i*.

While it is easy to focus solely on *p* and the bass line in this study, be sure the half-note durations of the upper notes are observed. A sloppy fingering or premature finger lift can compromise the legato of the upper line.

Frequently, left-hand fingers are held down while other fingers move to accommodate the bass line. This requires a heightened awareness of finger independence in the left hand. Measures 7 and 8 are good examples of this.

Special care should be taken to comply with the rests notated in measures 24, 25, 28, and 29. Carcassi requests the bass note be muted at the beginning of beat 2 in measure 24. If the bass note is fingered, as in measure 24, simply lift it up slightly but keep it in contact with the string. However, when bass notes are open strings, as in measure 25, *p* will have to touch the string to stop it from ringing. Specific awareness should be used when muting a bass note while playing a melody note at the same time (e.g., beat 3 of measure 25).

Performance Notes

"Etude No. 6" presents a musical structure of a bass-line melody with a chorale-like melody in the top voice. These two separate lines should complement each other. The player should strive to play the melody as legato as possible, while applying a focused and consistent tone on the top notes. In measure 9, the melody is transferred to the treble voice. The intention should remain the same here, with a legato melody and good tonal emphasis on the accompanying notes.

This etude is also a study in *upbeat phrasing*, which is a way of organizing melodic figures by grouping "weaker" upbeats with stronger downbeats to give the piece a sense of forward motion. An example of upbeat phrasing is grouping the last three notes of measure 2 with the first beat of measure 3. Groupings such as this are done through the use of articulation, dynamics, and rubato.

Etude No. 7

pg. 32

Purpose

"Etude No. 7" serves as a perfect introduction to tremolo technique. This etude also uses the technique of moving up and down the 1st string quickly, *i–a* alternation, and the *p–i–m–i* arpeggio. Additionally, the tempo marking of *Allegro* (one of only five etudes from Op. 60 marked to be played very quickly), challenges the player to develop skills at higher speeds.

Technical Issues

Tremolo is a *p–a–m–i* arpeggio where the fingers are completely sympathetic and alternate as a group with *p*. The *a*, *m*, and *i* fingers create a rapid repetition of a note on a single string, much like the quick down-up alternate-picking effect used on a mandolin.

---

13 *The Shearer Method*, Book 2 covers all five of the arpeggios without *p*, including *a–m–i–m*, which can be found on pg. 182.

In the *p–i–a–i* and *p–i–m–i*[14] arpeggios, make sure *m* and *a* are always moving sympathetically with an alternation occurring between *i* and *m*.

In measures 3–4 and 6–7, the 3rd finger of the left hand often remains depressed as other fingers move around it. This can present a finger-independence challenge, so practice this slowly at first, ensuring the 3rd finger remains stable.

Measures 16–19 include an *a–m–i* arpeggio,[15] which requires *m* and *a* to move sympathetically, alternating with *i*.

Use a metronome while building speed, and never sacrifice clarity for tempo.

The Shearer Perspective

Remember, when preparing a piece, it is very important to continually pre-read and "play and say" the selection to help develop strong habits of ADM.

Aaron Shearer would make sure all arpeggios and right-hand finger sequences are working correctly. Additionally, he would want all the down-stemmed notes, as well as the D♯ in measures 16–19, to be played with *p* in order to bring this line to the forefront. Interestingly, in the first edition, Carcassi stemmed the D♯ down in measure 17 and then up two measures later.

Performance Notes

The key to performing this etude well is making sure the tremolo pattern is rhythmically even. As the piece becomes more familiar, work towards increasing the tempo to make it more exciting for the listener. Musically, this piece has an aggressive style and can be performed animatedly. Balance between the bass and tremolo melody is also important.

Etude No. 8

pg. 34

Purpose

"Etude No. 8" is one of only two etudes in this collection that is in the key of E Major. Playing in the key of E Major can create some challenges for the player, such as adding the note D♯ to left-hand fingerings. Fixed-position slurs with appoggiaturas are the primary focuses of "Etude No. 8." The use of guide fingers is also prominent.

Technical Issues

The *brush slur*[16] is used in "Etude No. 8." After the slur is executed, the finger brushes lightly across the top of the next adjacent string. This creates a very even tone that sounds somewhere between the more-dominant rest slur and more-subtle free slur. Players should strive to maintain the same character of tone and volume in every slur.

Take note that guide fingers are found throughout this composition, starting in the transition from measure 1 to 2. While pre-reading the piece, highlight these guide fingers on the score to ensure security.

Although a four-string barre on I is not needed in measure 13, it is indicated for the following measure. Thus, if a four-string barre is utilized in measure 13, it will save the player from having to adjust for the barre in measures 14 and 15.

In the second beat of measure 23, the 1st finger of the left hand will go under the 2nd, thus creating what might feel like an awkward left-hand movement. Isolate this movement form to develop security.

All cadences in "Etude No. 8" end with an eighth-note rest.

The Shearer Perspective

"Etude No. 8" is another great piece for identifying triads. In lessons, Shearer would ask students to identify the triads and inversions by name. Each figure in this piece is a fixed triad with an appoggiatura. The third note of every four 16th-note grouping is the suspension, so the first, second, and fourth notes comprise the triad. Identifying these triads while pre-reading will better prepare the player to develop correct left-hand movements. Shearer would also encourage the use of ADM, especially during shifts.

Performance

In performance, pay special attention to the dynamic markings. Carcassi's dynamic markings support the building tension of the harmonic structure found in "Etude No. 8."

Etude No. 9

pg. 36

Purpose

While "Etude No. 8" focuses on pull-off slurs performed primarily by the 4th finger, "Etude No. 9" employs both pull-offs and hammer-ons with all the left-hand fingers.[17] In addition, "Etude No. 9" assists in the development of string-dampening technique with *p*.

---

14 *The Shearer Method*, Book 1, pg. 97 introduces the *p–i–m–i* arpeggio, while pg. 129 introduces the *p–i–a–i* arpeggio.

15 The *a–m–i* arpeggio is another arpeggio without *p* and is introduced in *The Shearer Method*, Book 2, pg. 123.

16 For more information on brush slurs, see *The Shearer Method*, Book 2, pg. 52 and the *Shearer Online Supplement*.

17 *The Shearer Method*, Book 2, pg. 52 includes a review of all types of slurs, including pull-offs and hammer-ons.

Technical Issues

Since this etude is slur-intensive, players should work to maintain an even sound among pull-offs and hammer-ons. The slurs in this etude move among various combinations of left-hand fingers, making consistency even more challenging. It is also important to highlight the technique of string dampening with *p*. An example of this dampening occurs in measure 2, where the following symbol • *p* • ⑤ appears. This symbol instructs the player to dampen the 5th string with *p* immediately after sounding the 6th string. Otherwise, the 5th string will continue to sound while the 6th string is played, which would make the bass unclear and harmonically incorrect. Practice this dampening technique as its own movement form; prepare *p* on the 6th string, then after sounding the 6th string, have *p* come to rest on the 5th string almost as if performing a rest stroke.[18] There is no reason to allow the hand to tilt outward into a clear *p* rest-stroke position. Instead, stay tilted inward toward the sound hole so that *p* maintains a free-stroke sound but mutes the 5th string by touching it.

Notice the indication at measure 9 to string cross when *p* moves to the 4th string. Make sure this string-crossing motion occurs from the right elbow.

Measures 13–15 present an interesting technique of combining a glissando and a slur. This can present a challenge for the player in terms of timing and coordination of the left hand.

The Shearer Perspective

Shearer's primary goal in this etude was to pre-read and "play and say" slowly. This would achieve increased accuracy while also reinforcing ADM. Initial slow work, to minimize confusion and error, would take priority over *continuity playing* (maintaining continuity) or consideration of a performance tempo.

Performance

Pay special attention to the harmonic tension and resolution present in "Etude No. 9." The active harmonic motion should inform the player's decisions related to phrasing. In addition, some of the slurs have been removed from the original manuscript for ease of performance.

---

18 A definition and demonstration of rest stroke for *p* and the fingers can be found in *The Shearer Method*, Book 2, pg. 2.

Etude No. 10

pg. 38

Purpose

The focus of "Etude No. 10" is rhythmic clarity of the triplet. Articulating the 16th-note triplets[19] in the time of one eighth note while maintaining even slurs presents a challenge. This study is also a great exercise for maintaining an even subdivision with the triplets and not allowing them to gallop or bounce. This etude also employs complex slurs that combine hammer-ons and pull-offs.

Technical Issues

In order to maintain smooth left-hand shifting, note the guide fingers throughout the piece. Notice how the 3rd finger of the left hand stays in contact with the 2nd string during the shift from measure 6 to measure 7. The same type of shift occurs at measure 14–15 and throughout the B section. Pay special attention to how the left hand looks in a mirror while shifting from position to position. If any jerkiness or hesitation occurs, isolate the specific movement to better understand the movement of the fingers. These shifting movements should be very smooth.

When playing an open 6th string followed by open 5th string, be sure to mute the lower open string so that it does not ring over. This muting can be achieved with the backside of the thumb as it prepares to play the next higher string.

In regard to the right hand in this etude, pay close attention to *i–m* when playing 3rds and *i–a* when playing 6ths. These fingers should be moving sympathetically and following through sufficiently to produce a round and powerful sound.

The Shearer Perspective

Shearer would use "Etude No. 10" as another opportunity to identify and analyze the chords used throughout the piece. Every other measure of this study can be summarized as one chord. This analysis can help with memorization and developing a deeper harmonic understanding of the piece.

Performance

A nice character can be achieved by applying a slight staccato to beats 2 and 3 in measure 2. This articulation can continue to be applied throughout the piece in similar measures, giving the etude a waltz-like lilt.

---

19 *The Shearer Method*, Book 3, pg. 40 defines triplets.

Etude No. 11

pg. 39

Purpose

Creating a musical dialogue or conversation between two voices should be a priority in "Etude No. 11." The main motif in this piece consists of four notes, three of which are pickups. This melody is answered by a countermelody, also consisting of four notes. These two lines create a dialogue between the top and bottom voices throughout "Etude No. 11." Being able to create the illusion of multiple voices or instruments is part of the beauty of the classical guitar. The guitar has the keen ability to articulate a melody with an accompaniment. To assist in creating this illusion, allow the first note of each measure to ring over the following accompaniment notes. To clearly hear this interplay between voices, play each one separately. Play the melody while imagining being accompanied by someone else. Then do the same for the accompaniment. Finally, put them both together to create the illusion of two separate instruments.

Technical Issues

Shearer's suggestion of holding the melody note on the downbeat longer creates substantial demand for finger independence in the left hand. Notice in measure 1 that the 4th finger must hold down D while the other fingers move around it. This kind of technical demand can bring left-hand deficiencies to the surface. A good approach would be to practice the "spider chord"[20] exercise or "parallel octave"[21] exercise from *The Shearer Method*. These activities emphasize and reinforce left-hand movement independence and help develop habits that will serve well in bringing out the beautiful melodic qualities of "Etude No. 11."

The Shearer Perspective

Right-hand finger consistency would be a primary concern for Shearer in this etude. The repeated use of *a–m–i–m*, *i–m–a–m*, or *p–i–m–p* is no accident and creates an opportunity to incorporate sympathetic motion for the purpose of note grouping. Check that the right-hand form is correct while executing these patterns.

Performance

Developing the ability to distinguish the two active voices in "Etude No. 11" will ultimately yield a great performance. Work to make each voice legato, and create a flow from these single-note lines. It would be easy to play this etude staccato or choppy, but it takes more control to connect the lines for longer phrases.

---

20 *The Shearer Method*, Book 2, pg. vi, video 10 presentation illustrates spider chords.
21 *The Shearer Method*, Book 3, pg. v introduces the parallel octave.

Etude No. 12

pg. 40

Purpose

The primary left-hand technique in "Etude No. 12" is positional shifting with the application of a half barre. Be careful not to gliss with the barre as you move it around the neck. This can be accomplished by carefully practicing the timing of the shift with the release of the barre. Also, pay special attention to when a barre must be lifted in order to effectively finger a subsequent measure.

Technical Issues

The *p–m–i–p* arpeggio in the right hand will require sympathetic motion between *m* and *i*. Proper attention should be given to good form and follow-through with *p*, which is continuously sounded as each sequence repeats. Measures 7, 8, and 20 require a thumb mute. In these measures, while sounding the bass string, *p* must simultaneously mute the next lower adjacent string. This muting is achieved at the moment that *p* prepares. While placing *p* to sound the 4th string, allow the side of the thumb to touch and mute the 5th string. This muting will allow the bass line to be clear and not leave unwanted voices ringing to create incorrect harmonies.

An important left-hand event occurs between measure 12 and 13: The B Minor chord on beat 4 of measure 20 has the 2nd finger on D. Be sure to lift the 2nd finger early enough to prepare it for the E at the downbeat of measure 21. The B, held by the 1st finger, will act as a pivot to assist in achieving this movement without sounding staccato.

Notice also the use of a hinge barre[22] at the end of this etude in measure 20.

The Shearer Perspective

Pre-reading with "play and say," as well as chord recognition, will benefit the player while studying "Etude No. 12."

Performance

Be sure to bring out the dotted-bass melody that exists throughout this etude. Holding the dotted eighth and grouping the 16th so that it connects to the following downbeat should be a priority. This will enhance the feeling of downbeat phrasing.

---

22 *The Shearer Method*, Book 3, pg. 66 introduces the hinge barre. An additional video is available at the *Shearer Online Supplement*.

Etude No. 13

pg. 42

Purpose

"Etude No. 13" provides another great opportunity for the player to reinforce two right-hand movement forms: *p–i–m* and *a–m–i*. Additionally, analysis of the triads in this etude will offer a deeper understanding of the harmonic structure.

Technical Issues

While playing *p–i–m–a*, be sure that *i–m–a* are working sympathetically. As *a* plays, extend *m* and *i* simultaneously to create an alternation movement. The *i* finger should move with *m*, and *c* (pinky) should move with *a* during this alternation. Working with a mirror can help ensure this movement is happening correctly. Note a change in the right-hand arpeggio at measure 7 due to a different string grouping.

"Etude No. 13" also contains numerous examples of guide shifts. Be sure to hold the left-hand finger (the one that is common to where you begin and end the shift) down. These guide shifts will assist the left hand with moving up and down the neck. It is important to clarify where the notes are located on the score and on the fretboard. These are great opportunities for the player to apply ADM and to see ahead as a shift is occurring.

The Shearer Perspective

Pre-reading will help clarify accurate progress with this study.

Performance

There is wonderful opportunity with triad and chord identification to add a lot of musical expression when playing this etude. The harmonic movement offers the player several options for added expressive tools such as crescendos, decrescendos, and other dynamic changes.

Etude No. 14

pg. 44

Purpose

The purpose of this etude is rooted in *i–m* alternation in the context of scale work. The scale passages in this piece require focused left- and right-hand work, including string crossing, shifting, and legato practice. The technical level of this etude is more demanding because it requires detailed coordination and speed of both hands.

Technical Issues

On beat 1 of measure 2, the 4th finger is positioned on the 5th string while the 3rd finger is on 4th string. This position can feel awkward unless you rotate the forearm clockwise while bring the elbow slightly in towards your torso. This allows the hand and arm to yield to the pull of the fingers, which is a natural tool for the left hand.

The Shearer Perspective

Shearer raised the bar technically in this etude by making the bass note a quarter note followed by a quarter rest. Carcassi's original manuscript had half notes in the bass, which allowed the bass to ring through. By altering the bass notes to a single beat, bass muting becomes an intensive activity in "Etude No. 14." Thumb muting is a movement form that involves the entire right hand. For example, in the first measure, while sounding the C♯ with *i*, *p* simultaneously prepares on ④. Practice by isolating this movement without the left hand until you feel comfortable.

In measures 10, 12, 24, and 26, Shearer altered the top notes to be held over the bass line. He believed this created a more-realistic illusion of two instruments playing simultaneously.

Performance

It's important to articulate the polyphonic dialogue between voices in "Etude No. 14." Strive for legato and long lines when considering phrasing. It is easy for guitarists to gravitate towards a staccato sound when playing scales or many single notes in a row. It is important to become aware of the larger phrases, especially when they are made up of individual scales.

Etude No. 15

pg. 46

Purpose

The alternation of *i* and *m* is the fundamental technical theme in "Etude No. 15." While seeking to emphasize the melody, it is important to identify the role of each finger. The *p* finger sounds the bass and creates the foundation for this etude, while *i* plays the inner voice of the chord. This arrangement creates an accompaniment very similar to an *Alberti bass* (accompaniment figure derived from broken chords) often found in Classical-era accompaniment. Finally, the *m* finger is left with the responsibility of sounding the melody. Pay close attention to the attack and volume of each finger to create an illusion of multiple instruments or voices.

Technical Issues

Work in front of a mirror to ensure that the *i–m* alternation is working correctly. The *a* finger should always move with *m*. Logically, the *m* finger should move with *a* in the same manner. String crossing is a vital aspect of the right hand in this piece. For example, the first three groupings of the etude's eight-note arpeggio figure occur over three different sets of strings (4th–3rd, 3rd–2nd, 2nd–1st). Be sure to move the right forearm from the elbow, maintaining a secure wrist and hand position while negotiating the move from one string set to the next. Identify other places within this etude where string crossing takes place.

In order to take advantage of the natural relationship between the spacing of the right-hand fingers and the strings, utilize *a* in measures 7 and 9. Using *a* here is more comfortable than *m* and negates the need for a string crossing.

The Shearer Perspective

While Carcassi did not notate the melody notes in this etude as eighths ringing over the accompaniment, it is most likely implied. Shearer added eighth-note stemming to the melody, so the player can intentionally create a legato melody that will ring over the accompanying notes.

Performance

"Etude No. 15" is a beautiful piece that provides multiple rises in melody and active harmonic changes. There are many opportunities for crescendos, decrescendos, and breaths through the judicious use of rubato.

Etude No. 16

pg. 48

Purpose

"Etude No. 16" provides a clear opportunity for the player to emphasize the melody while softening the accompanying, or inner, voices. This technique is common for guitarists, as the right-hand fingers are often required to differentiate between melody and accompaniment. "Etude No. 16" is the only etude in this collection in the key of F Major, which makes for some interesting and unique left-hand chords and shapes. This study demands a specific use of legato by holding melodies over several eighth-note accompaniments.

Technical Issues

A clear melody with accompaniment is established in "Etude No. 16." It is beneficial to isolate the melody (stems up) to hear how it would be stated if that was the only part being played. Take care to maintain a connected and legato melodic line when adding in the accompanying notes.

A common mishap in this piece is cutting off the last note of the accompaniment directly before a shift. Be sure to time the shift so that the note prior to moving does not sound staccato.

Measures 2 and 4 use hinge barres to assist in smooth finger transitions. Note that measure 2 is an upward hinge barre, while in measure 4 it is downward.

In measures 6–8, we use a guide shift (4th finger) on the 1st string. This occurs again in measures 15–18.

The Shearer Perspective

While Carcassi did not include right-hand fingerings in this etude, some earlier editions indicated the use of *i*, *m*, and *a*. This fingering would place an alternation between *m* and *a*. While it is good to be equally fluent with *m–a* alternation, Shearer believed it would be more prudent to sound the notes with *p*, *i*, and *m*. This places the alternation between the *i* and *m* fingers, which is easier than alternating with *m* and *a*. As the player grows more comfortable with the etude, the right-hand fingering *i*, *m*, and *a* can be applied to reinforce fluency of the *m–a* alternation. Establishing an equal fluency with alternations between all finger combinations will ultimately help the player develop greater freedom in the right hand and reduce tension.

Performance

Work to balance the melody and accompaniment while making sure the *a* finger has the best tone possible on the top voice. Be particularly mindful of Carcassi's dynamic markings as they provide detailed cues about harmonic motion.

Etude No. 17

pg. 50

Purpose

"Etude No. 17" is a complex technical study that uses octaves, 10ths, and open intervals in linear passages moving up and down the fingerboard. Connecting melodic lines in both voices in this etude is challenging. This study's unique voice separation gives students a chance to develop greater flexibility and accuracy with *p* as it moves between bass and treble strings. Carcassi offered no right-hand fingerings; Shearer suggested a *p–i–p–m* alternation pattern.

Technical Issues

Before approaching "Etude No. 17," it might be helpful to revisit the spider chord and parallel-octave exercises suggested in "Etude No. 11," Technical Issues (page 10). This will help develop a higher level of finger independence and skill required for this study. When first approaching these exercises, focus on keeping the left palm parallel to the fretboard, thus placing emphasis on the finger's ability to reach for notes. Furthermore, allow the left arm and hand to yield to the pull of the fingers when needed. This will enable the elbow to move slightly inward and outward in relation to your torso, making the movement forms in "Etude No. 17" easier.

The Shearer Perspective

Shearer would make sure there was consistency with the *p–i–p–m* sequence, except for measures 38–42 where deviation from this pattern is indicated. He would also urge that any *i–m–a* or *a–m–i* sequence utilize sympathetic movement.

Shearer suggested the chords in measures 39–43 could be played with a *p* sweep. In order for the sweep to be even and smooth, tilt the hand outward slightly and sweep downward with *p* by rotating the forearm and moving from the elbow. This *p* sweep technique can yield a full and rich sound. Shearer added a slur in measure 44 and a tie on the 5th-string E from measure 44 to 45.

Performance

Strive to make the shifts in "Etude No. 17" as legato as possible. Carcassi marked strong dynamic entrances with diminuendos at the end of each phrase with the exception of the coda and ending. Players should develop a keen sense of dynamic control over two-measure phrases and throughout each eight-measure period. Work on this etude slowly with a metronome to build to a performance tempo gradually over time.

Etude No. 18

pg. 52

Purpose

Carcassi introduces downward shifting on the 1st string to coincide with a quick triplet melodic sequence. This study presents several opportunities to practice and apply bass muting. Reminiscent of "Etude No. 2," Carcassi includes a few opportunities for the player to work on *a–m* alternation in this study.

Technical Issues

Memorization and ADM are both important tools to help with the shifts in this etude. Be conscious of the fret numbers and note names where the shifts occur. Applying "say and play" will clarify and enhance the memory process to build confidence. Be aware of which shifts are half and whole steps, as some require a reach (e.g., beats 4, 5, and 6 of measure 1).

Measures 2, 3, 15, 16, 32, 34, and 35 require specific bass notes to be muted. Additional muting is required in measures 5–8 where the harmonies switch between A Major and D Major with the roots on open bass notes. From the onset, take time to mark the score in places where bass notes require muting, and practice the muting technique consciously throughout.

Applying a hinge barre (H.B.) at the end of measure 19 prevents the F♯ from ringing over the B in measure 20. As the B is played, release the fingertip so the F♯ is muted.

Measure 43 employs an *acciaccatura* with *grace notes* (small notes used to show an embellishment) on the downbeat.[23] The low E bass note is played simultaneously with the chord on the downbeat and is followed by a quick gliss with the 4th finger to the high D. Since acciaccatura means to "crush in," play the grace notes as quickly as possible without taking time from the melodic note.

The Shearer Perspective

Notice the string crossing between *a* and *m* at measures 19 and 23. Shearer would make sure this crossing occurred consciously and from the elbow.

Although Carcassi did not indicate any slurs in "Etude No. 18," Shearer did insert slurs that he felt added to the character of the study by creating legato and imparting a more *Allegretto* (lively) feel. If you choose to apply these slurs, make sure each slurred figure has the same character as the one before it. It's important to pay attention to the consistency of the hammer-ons.

Of course, Shearer's addition of slurs also affected his right-hand fingerings. As stated earlier in this edition, once comfortable using *i–m* alternation, Shearer would encourage *a–m* alternation. This would give additional practice for fluency with both fingering combinations.

Performance

Performing triplets quickly and evenly while maintaining legato is especially difficult. Shifting down the neck requires keen control of the guide finger as it moves from one position to another.

---

23 For more information on acciaccaturas and grace notes, see *The Shearer Method*, Book 2, pg. 189 or *Classic Guitar Technique: Supplement 1*, pg. 23

Etude No. 19

Purpose

"Etude No. 19" offers the player the opportunity to develop and reinforce the *a–m–i–m* arpeggio. Additionally important is the ability to distinguish between melody and accompaniment in this study.

pg. 54

Technical Issues

The melody in this etude is always articulated with *a*, thus requiring a slight emphasis on this finger while softening the inner voices of the arpeggio.

The 2nd finger plays an important transitional role in measures 18 and 22. Replace the 1st finger on the C with the 2nd finger, and move 1 to the A♯ in the bass on the third beat of measure 18. Likewise, repeat the same finger substitution on the third beat of measure 22.

In measures 28–31, the 2nd finger should be held down as a pivot finger. This will allow the 1st finger to move easily between the 1st and 5th strings.

As you practice measure 24, be sure to count aloud the subdivision of eighth notes.

The Shearer Perspective

A common problem regarding the right hand is an *a* side-pull away from *m*. A side-pull is awkward and can cause issues with accuracy and tone. Work in front of a mirror to make sure *a* flexes in a straight trajectory.[24]

Many of the aforementioned left-hand fingerings for this study are unique and originate from Shearer. Additionally, he would carefully observe the right-hand arpeggio, making sure *a* and *m* were always moving sympathetically.

Performance

"Etude No. 19" is written in two-measure binary phrases with clear antecedent-consequent symmetry. Performers should be aware of the longer phrases in every period and breathe every four measures to establish a structural balance. Carcassi noticeably raises the dynamic level of measures 21–34, marking *sf* in the downbeats of measures 23, 28, 29, 30, and 33. Players are encouraged to explore the limits of the dynamic level by increasing contact pressure with tip joints and releasing with a robust follow-through.

One of the joys of playing the classical guitar is the sound it makes. Focus on the most full *a* finger tone possible and make the melody sing.

Etude No. 20

Purpose

"Etude No. 20" is a complex and fast-paced compound quadruple-meter study in triplets. It includes quick-ascending arpeggios using open-string shifts and string crossings that demand exacting control and timing.

pg. 56

Technical Issues

Many measures in "Etude No. 20" include an arpeggio that requires string crossings to achieve the proper string grouping. Be sure all string crossings initiate from the elbow. Moving across strings, often from the 6th string to the 1st, is a challenge for the right hand. This study is an excellent precursor to a study like "Etude No. 2" by Villa-Lobos, where this technique is explored in depth.

Be aware of any guide shifts that will assist you in comfortably navigating the neck, such as the transitions in measures 23–24.

Guitarists sometimes tend to accentuate the note prior to a slur, which, in this context, is often the highest note in the arpeggio. Work to create an even and balanced sound when approaching slurs.

The Shearer Perspective

When comparing editions of Carcassi etudes, one will notice adjustments made by Shearer to maintain the consistency of slurs from phrase to phrase. Generally, the slurs occur from the first eighth note to the second and at the top of the arpeggio on beats 7 and 8.

Shearer suggests the player experiment with the use of rest stroke on the final note (high A) in this study for clarity and accentuation.

Performance

The most important point of this study is maintaining a legato feel while phrasing accurately in six-note groupings. Practice slowly at first, isolating right-hand arpeggios on open strings and gradually building to a performance tempo with a metronome. Distinguish where *p* has the melody by playing the accompanying arpeggios more softly, as in measures 11–12 and 14–16. "Etude No. 20" is a useful daily study and functions as an excellent companion to "Etude No. 25."

---

24   *The Shearer Method*, Book 1, pg. 137 demonstrates how to correct a side-pull.

Etude No. 21

pg. 58

Purpose

"Etude No. 21" is an excellent exercise for the execution of acciaccaturas and mordents, which ornament the primary musical motif and are found in almost every measure. The other notable technique required for this piece is the ability to shift chords quickly and accurately with the left hand. These two technical challenges make "Etude No. 21" an excellent left-hand study.

Technical Issues

Players must strive to successfully articulate the grace note figures by making the hammer-on, or pull-off, combinations sound consistent. Consistency should exist both in tone and rhythm of the grace notes throughout the piece, regardless of the fingering.[25]

There are many chances to apply specific tools to aid the left hand in landing chords accurately. These tools include ADM, shaping the chord in the air during the shift, practicing breaking apart the chord, guide fingers, controlling left-hand position, and holding down a finger to assist in placing a chord (e.g., measure 4).

Memorization would help tremendously with clean execution of this etude. This study is an excellent precursor to Fernando Sor's "Etude No. 20," Op. 31. The left hand will benefit from hinge barres at measures 25, 44, and 46. Notice these barres keep the 1st finger from having to jump or hop across strings.

String grouping of the right hand is uniquely important in this study. Some chords are sounded with *p–i–m* while others use *p–i–a*. The arpeggio is determined by the string grouping required to play the chord. If a chord is sounded with *p–i–m*, the phrase should start with *m* to properly set up the fingering sequence (e.g., the first pickup and measure of the piece). If the chord is sounded with *p–i–a*, the pickup for the phrase will be sounded with *a* (e.g., measure 3). These right-hand fingerings ensure alternation is occurring. While alternation may not always be possible, we should work to minimize the repetition of fingers in the right hand.

The Shearer Perspective

Shearer would have his students pre-read and "play and say" the fingerings of both hands to ensure flawless and accurate execution.

Performance

"Etude No. 21" is a light and spirited piece. The grace notes add lift and lilt to the phrasing and are first presented in the context of a major key. A key change to A Minor in measure 17 offers an opportunity to create musical contrast. Players can implement expressive devices (i.e., dynamics, color, and volume) to relay a contrasting mood during the minor section. Strive for clean and smooth execution of the grace notes and mordents, while maintaining even phrasing balance.

Etude No. 22

pg. 60

Purpose

"Etude No. 22" is a difficult technical study that demands rapid traveling across the six strings with both hands. The technique of crossing strings in this etude is achieved through both arpeggios and scales. While Carcassi introduced ascending arpeggios in "Etude No. 20," he focused primarily on descending arpeggios in "Etude No. 22."

Technical Issues

Barring is a challenge presented in this study (especially if using Shearer's fingerings in this edition). Work on barre placement, maintaining pressure only on the necessary strings while using gravity and the weight of the arm to help with pressure on the strings.

"Etude No. 22" mixes arpeggio forms with alternation in the right hand. It is important to differentiate between sympathetic and alternating movements. Balancing the sound of scales and arpeggios to achieve the same legato and dynamic flow can be difficult.

The use of *p* rest stroke to sweep the ascending arpeggio on the bass strings in the two section endings (measures 7–8 and 33–34) is recommended here. After sweeping two- and three-note groups, one must carefully adjust rotation to play the treble strings that follow.

In most cases, consideration of cross fingerings has been applied in right-hand fingerings. In some instances, however, awkward string crossings cannot be avoided. Mark these spots in the score to ensure awareness of the issue and enable accurate crossing.

It is imperative to apply good habits of pre-reading and "playing and saying" as the music becomes more challenging. A high frequency of mistakes is an indication that a slower tempo and the isolating of smaller sections are required.

Take the time needed to master this etude. Do not rush the process.

---

25 *The Shearer Method*, Book 3, pg. iv features a hammer-on/pull-off slur exercise.

The Shearer Perspective

Shearer incorporates *a–m–i–p* and *p–i–m–a* arpeggios, but these are integrated with *i–m* alternation and preceded many times with an *m–a* alternation and string crossing.

Shearer also works to eliminate awkward shifts through creative left-hand fingerings. For example, the opening measure in the 5th position uses a stretch with finger substitution to avoid crossing from the 5th string to the 1st with the 4th finger. This fingering solution also eliminates the leap from open-position C to the high C (F chord) in 5th position and keeps the tone color more consistent.

Performance

Technical issues aside, this etude becomes even more challenging when attempting to integrate the quickly changing, and frequent, dynamic markings. In most cases, when the line is descending, a decrescendo is utilized, and when ascending, a crescendo is utilized. While this effect will be an added challenge for the player, it captures Carcassi's expressive intentions and makes this study musically engaging.

Etude No. 23

pg. 62

Purpose

"Etude No. 23" is an advanced-level study involving pull-offs to open strings, slurs, complex right-hand fingerings, and fast scales. Although the purpose of upper-level Carcassi studies ("Etudes No. 19" to "25") in this collection is multi-dimensional, "Etude No. 23" focuses explicitly on open-string pull-offs and melodic shifting, techniques introduced in "Etude No. 7."

Technical Issues

While some of the right-hand fingerings tend to look like arpeggio forms, these fingerings are employed to assist in handling string-grouping transitions and to promote phrasing of note groupings.

In the left hand, many guide shifts and open-string transitions are used to seamlessly transition to various positions. A good example of open-string shifting can be found in measure 2, where the open 1st string is utilized to facilitate a shift from 9th to 1st position. The right-hand fingering during this shift uses *i–m–a* and *a–m–i* sympathetic movement forms, which help connect the change in string groupings from 3rd–2nd–1st to 4th–3rd–2nd. Measure 12 presents a similar situation.

Notice the downbeat of measure 29. Here, *m* assists in changing the string grouping for that measure so that the *p–i* alternation can transition the right hand from the 4th string to the 6th.

The level of intricacy in this piece is challenging and places multiple technical demands on the player. Allow plenty of time to learn and develop this piece.

The Shearer Perspective

Many of the aforementioned fingerings in the Technical Issues section for this piece involve Shearer's alternate left- and right-hand fingerings.

As the reader has likely gleaned, Shearer might add or remove a slur for a couple of reasons. His first priority would be to maintain consistency in phrasing or note grouping. Another would be to maintain better flow with an alternate left-hand fingering that does not allow for the slur. Refer to measures 2 and 4.

Performance

Pull-offs from a fretted note to an open string require keen awareness and control, especially with the timing and velocity of the pull-off finger as it plucks to the open string. This is especially true when pulling off from a 2nd-string fretted note to the open string while also holding a bass note. Carefully visualize the position of the ascending shifts and the fret distance between the notes. This will help establish a reliable sense of space while ascending and descending on the same string. As this study becomes more fluent, experiment with the tempo, using a metronome, to develop even execution of pull-offs at higher speeds. Remember that *Allegro* can be achieved with a wide range of metronome markings.

Etude No. 24

pg. 64

Purpose

"Etude No. 24" uses an accumulation of techniques presented in previous etudes in this collection. Set in a complex rhythmic context, players are challenged with grace-note embellishments, chords, scale work, slurs, and quick 32nd-note mordents.

Technical Issues

The rhythmic nature of "Etude No. 24" provides an opportunity to solidify the practice of subdividing the beat and clarifying complex rhythms. Fortunately, there are guide shifts throughout this etude to help make shifting and transitions easier. A few of these examples can be found in measures 1, 10, 12, and 39.

The acciaccatura (e.g., measure 5) might require some special attention during practice. Remember these notes occur on the beat and resolve to the principal note.

The clever use of sympathetic motion can be applied in many places throughout the piece and is illustrated immediately in measures 1, 2, and 3. Playing the 32nd-note pickup and the downbeat with alternation can be tricky. By using sympathetic motion with *a–m* or *m–a*, the quick notes will be much easier to play evenly and fluently. Flex *a* and *m* together in preparation to play the final note (or pickup note) in measure 2.

The Shearer Perspective

Shearer often made choices about position on the fretboard according to tone or color. While playing the first few measures of "Etude No. 24" in open position would be easier, Shearer places the opening melodic lines on the 2nd and 3rd strings. This allows players to highlight the fuller and warmer texture of the 2nd string. Often, Shearer would remove open strings in melodic shifting in order to keep consistent color and vibrato on a single string. In order to accomplish this legato, a player must contemplate and prioritize note groupings according to phrasing. It can be a valuable lesson to consider this study from a new perspective, placing tone and movement of the melodic line above technical ease.

Due to the rhythmic complexity found in this etude, Shearer would ask the player to conduct the beat and count aloud, making sure the 32nd-note dot was precise and the descending triplet line square on the eighth notes (e.g., measures 4–7).

Though both *a–m* and *i–m* are offered as possible alternations, *i–m* might be the better choice for fluency in the context of a performance.

Performance

This beautiful and stately piece offers many opportunities for coloristic effects, dynamic mirroring, and rubato phrasing. The B section, in particular, shifts the melody to *p* in the bass. Be sure to bring out the bass line while softening accompanying chords/notes. Sing the melody to aid with shaping and applying rubato.

Etude No. 25

pg. 68

Purpose

"Etude No. 25" is perhaps the most technically demanding study in *25 Etude Mélodiques*. This piece reinforces many of the techniques found in this edition's previous etudes and functions as a virtuosic grand finale for Op. 60. Open-string position changes, numerous and varying shifts, left-hand finger substitution, as well as arpeggio forms and alternation, are written throughout the four pages of this study, constituting the longest piece in the collection. Without a doubt, Carcassi's tempo indication, *Allegro Brilliante*, will challenge performers to develop sustained control and speed.

Technical Issues

Establishing clear guides and indicators for positional shifting is essential while starting to read and visualize this study. At first glance, some left-hand fingerings may seem odd or non-traditional. However, they exist for the purpose of setting the hand in position for an upcoming finger grouping or placement. An example of this can be found in beat 4 of measure 9. The final note in that measure (C) is played with the 4th finger, which leaves the 3rd finger free to access the upcoming G on the downbeat of the following measure. Another example of a clever left-hand fingering exists in measure 14, when C is played with the 4th finger. This fingering enables the upcoming A Minor chord to be easily executed.

All but one positional change in this etude can be accomplished by using an open string to make the shift. Using open strings to shift enables a more legato sound and mitigates unnecessary movements. Players must be mindful to adjust tone on open strings, which tend to sound louder and have a tendency to stick out.

One shift that is an exception to open-string shifting can be found in measure 6, beat 3. A 4–2–3–1 shift occurs to transition from 9th position to 7th (IX to VII). This is a very compact way of shifting through two positions and is commonly applied in comprehensive scale studies.[26] This shift occurs at the half step between the 2nd and 3rd fingers.

Always clarify right-hand fingerings to distinguish alternation versus sympathetic motion.

The Shearer Perspective

Shearer would encourage the player to work with "Etude No. 25" in small sections, one measure at a time or even breaking it down into smaller movements. Pre-reading and "playing and saying" in single-measure increments will assist you in minimizing confusion and error. When pre-reading, begin by clarifying the rhythm, then say letter and finger names (left and right) aloud.

As in previous etudes, Shearer removed or altered placement of slurs in "Etude No. 25" to maintain phrase consistency. In Shearer's manuscript, the downbeat, as well as the turnaround at the highest note of the sequence, will be slurred.

At measure 36, Shearer changes the notes to resemble measure 38 as opposed to measure 34. This was his personal preference in the development of the line.

---

26   *The Shearer Method*, Book 3, pg. 236 covers comprehensive scales, both major and minor.

Performance

Be mindful that this study indicates general dynamic markings f, ff, and sf. Observe the brisk dynamic changes in measures 2, 4, 10, 12, 30, and 32. At high speed, these quick changes require exceptional control. Due to the open string slurs and dampened bass notes, the coda (measure 46) is perhaps the trickiest section to execute evenly at a *forte* dynamic.

"Etude No. 25" is a delightful and fun piece to play at fast tempos. The rewards of spending time on a piece like this are great. Do not be in a hurry to get up to performance tempo. Ultimately, *Allegro Brilliante* is determined by the player's ability. Pushing the limits without sacrificing accuracy is the key to making the music work on a high level.

About the Editors and Performance Notes Authors

Thomas Kikta is a versatile artist as a classical guitarist, vocalist, composer, pedagogue, producer, and author. He has been the director of classical guitar and recording arts and sciences at Duquesne University in Pittsburgh, PA for over 30 years. Working closely with Aaron Shearer for over 28 years, he co-authored with Shearer the third edition of the best selling *Classic Guitar Technique*, Volume 1 and *The Shearer Method*. Kikta is co-founder and vice president of the Aaron Shearer Foundation.

Dr. Kami Rowan is a nationally known guitar pedagogue and an associate professor at Guilford College. Her graduates have attended some of the most prestigious graduate music programs in the United States. Dr. Rowan also worked collaboratively to create a magnet high school and curriculum, and received her NC-A Teaching license from the University of NC at Greensboro. Dr. Rowan is the director of the Eastern Music Festival guitar program, president of the Piedmont Classic Guitar Society, and co-founder of the Aaron Shearer Foundation.

Ricardo Cobo began his studies with Aaron Shearer at the Peabody Institute. He earned his B.M. from The University of North Carolina School of the Arts and M.M. from Florida State University, where he later became a doctoral fellow. Winner of the Guitar Foundation of America's Solo International Competition, Cobo has recorded extensively for Naxos, Angel/Emi, Essay, Ellipsis, and Cambria. Cobo is director of classic guitar studies at University of Nevada, Las Vegas (UNLV), co-founder of the UNLV/Allegro Guitar Series, president of GuitarLasVegas.org, and co-founder of the Aaron Shearer Foundation.

A Note from the Publisher

We are proud to present Alfred's Classical Guitar Masterwork Editions. Our goal is to provide classical guitar students and performers the best possible editions of important repertoire with the editorial perspectives of great artists and teachers. The fingerings and other technical guides included in these scores will give you not only what may be new windows from which to view the pieces, but new views into the thinking of these great artists and teachers of classical guitar.

The pieces, of course, do not live on these pages. It is you who will breathe life into them and embue them with meaning. Thus, it is important that you learn everything you can about the composers and their intent, the styles and conventions of the periods and regions in which they were composed, and all of the formal aspects of their structures. A great performance is, among other things, well-informed.

In the end, you must make your own choices about fingerings, articulations, dynamics, phrasing, etc.—all of which are integrally related. Everything in the volume you're holding now is from a respected classical guitarist's view of the music, but we encourage you to dig deeper and go further—research, experiment, discuss, and become intimate with everything about the pieces you choose to study and perform. This is one of the great joys of being a musician: Music is not static; it lives and breathes in the work you do.

Thank you for including our edition in your study.

–Nathaniel Gunod, Alfred Music

Aaron Shearer
1919–2008

Etude No. 1  Track 1

Etude No. 2

Track 2

*Ossia:

etc.   Alternate performance: Track 26

Etude No. 3

Track 3

Etude No. 4 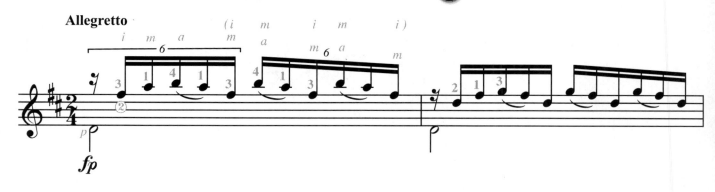 Track 4

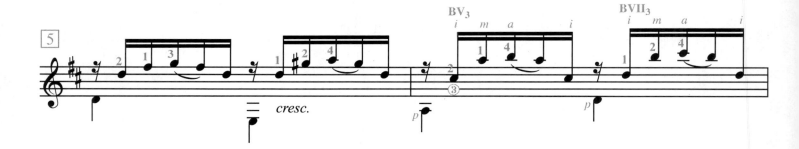

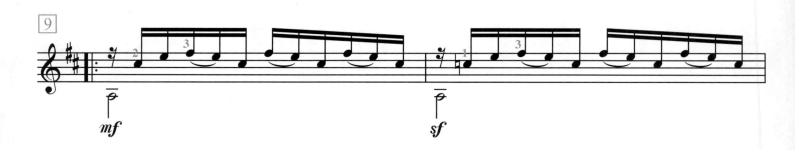

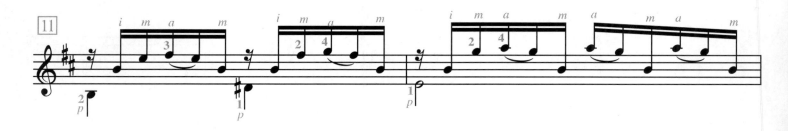

Etude No. 5  Track 5

Etude No. 6 🔊 Track 6

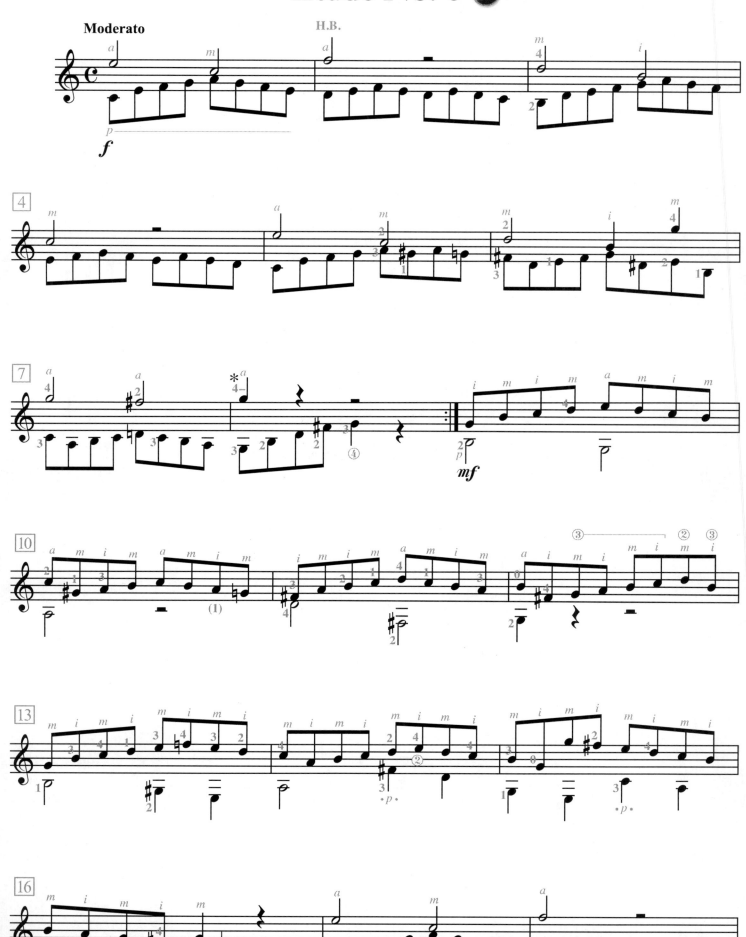

*phantom guide
  see page 7: "Etude No. 6," Technical Issues

Etude No. 7  Track 7

Etude No. 8  Track 8

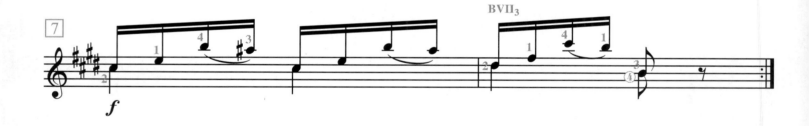

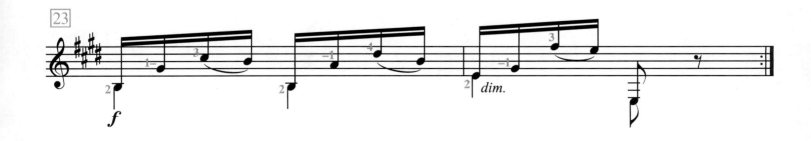

Etude No. 9  Track 9

Etude No. 10

Track 10

Allegretto

Etude No. 11  Track 11

Etude No. 12 🔊 Track 12

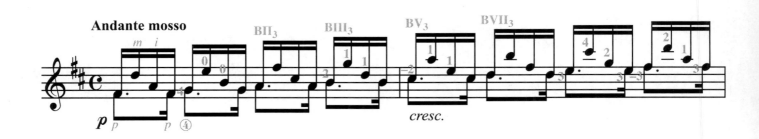

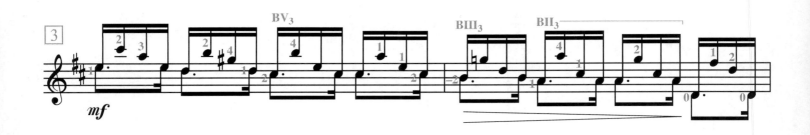

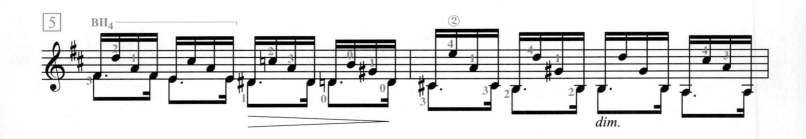

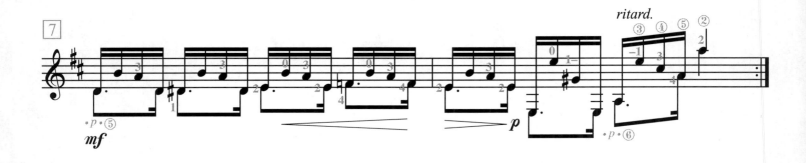

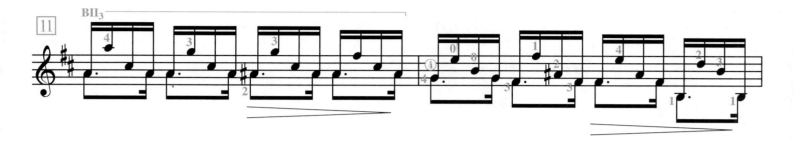

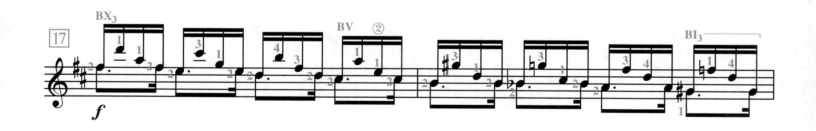

Etude No. 13

Track 13

Etude No. 14  Track 14

46

Etude No. 15 Track 15

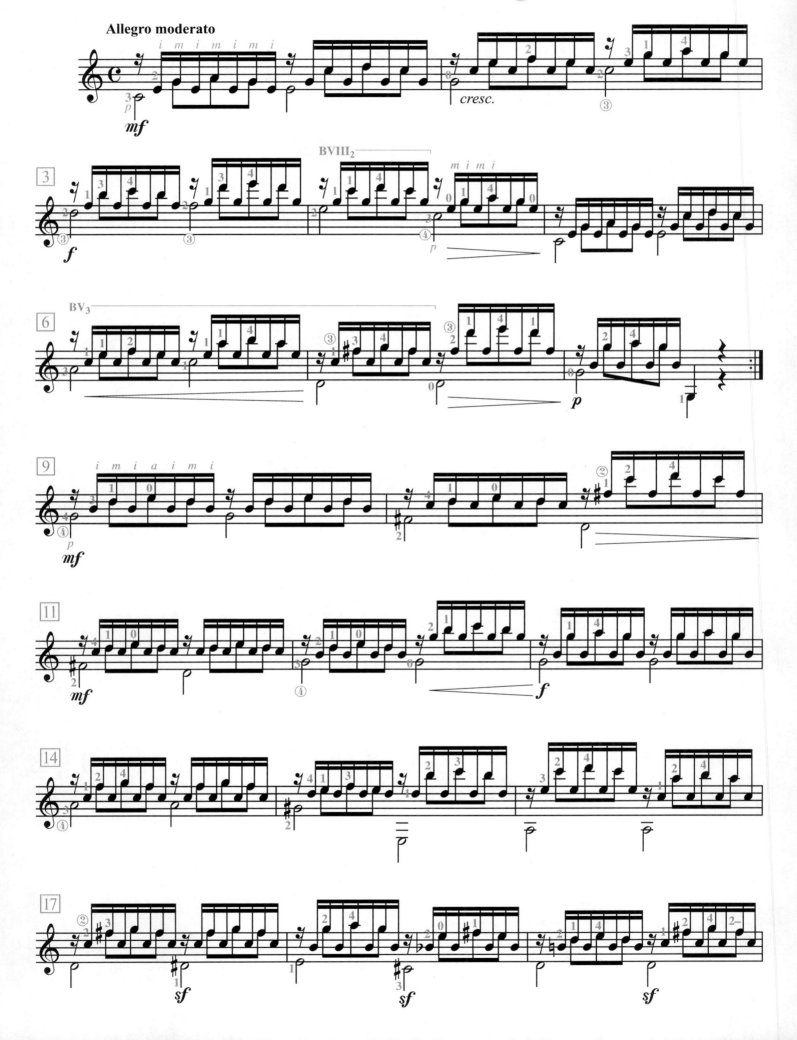

47

Etude No. 16

Track 16

This page intentionally left blank by the publisher.

Etude No. 17

Track 17

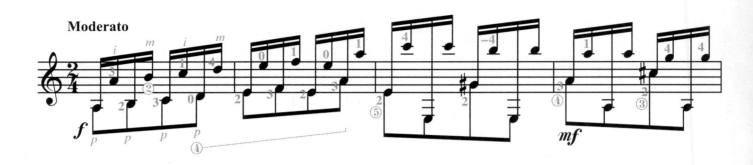

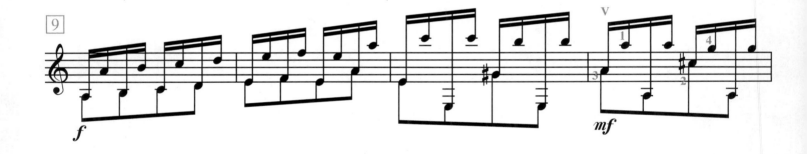

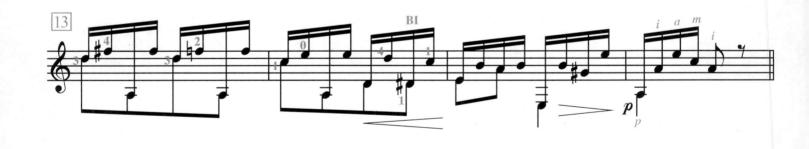

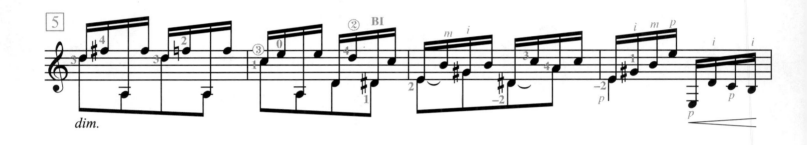

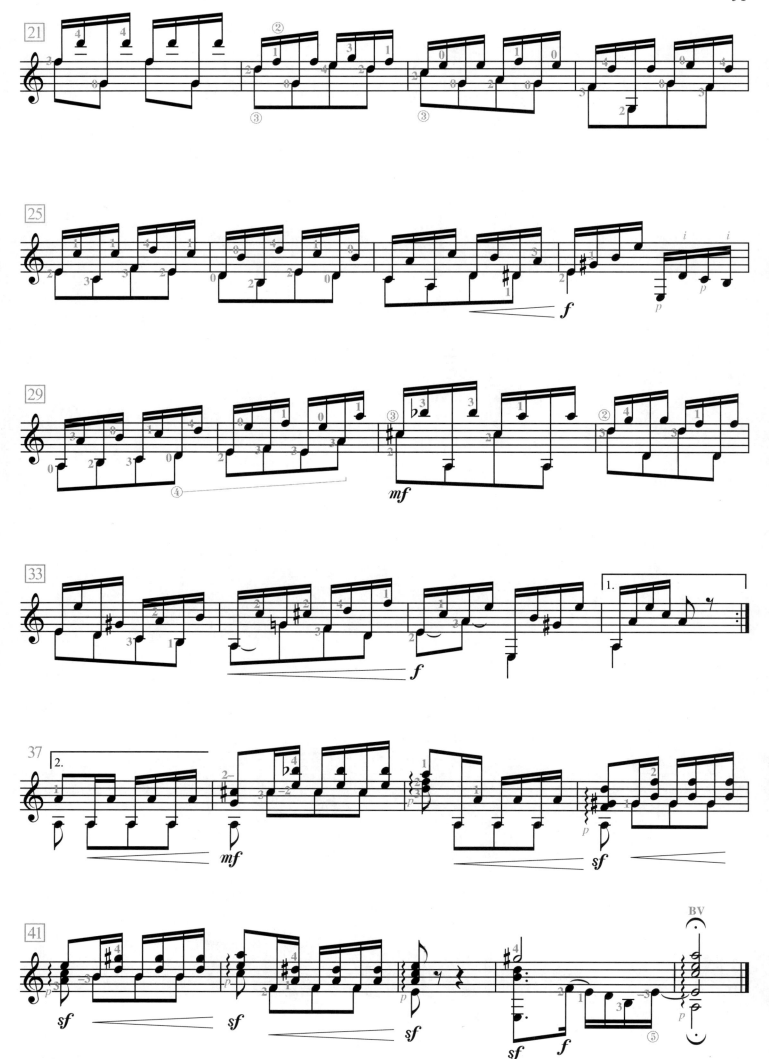

Etude No. 18

54

Etude No. 19 🔊 Track 19

Etude No. 20  Track 20

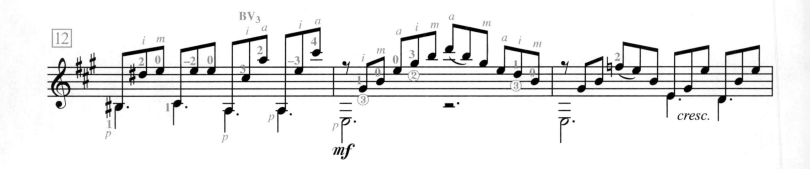

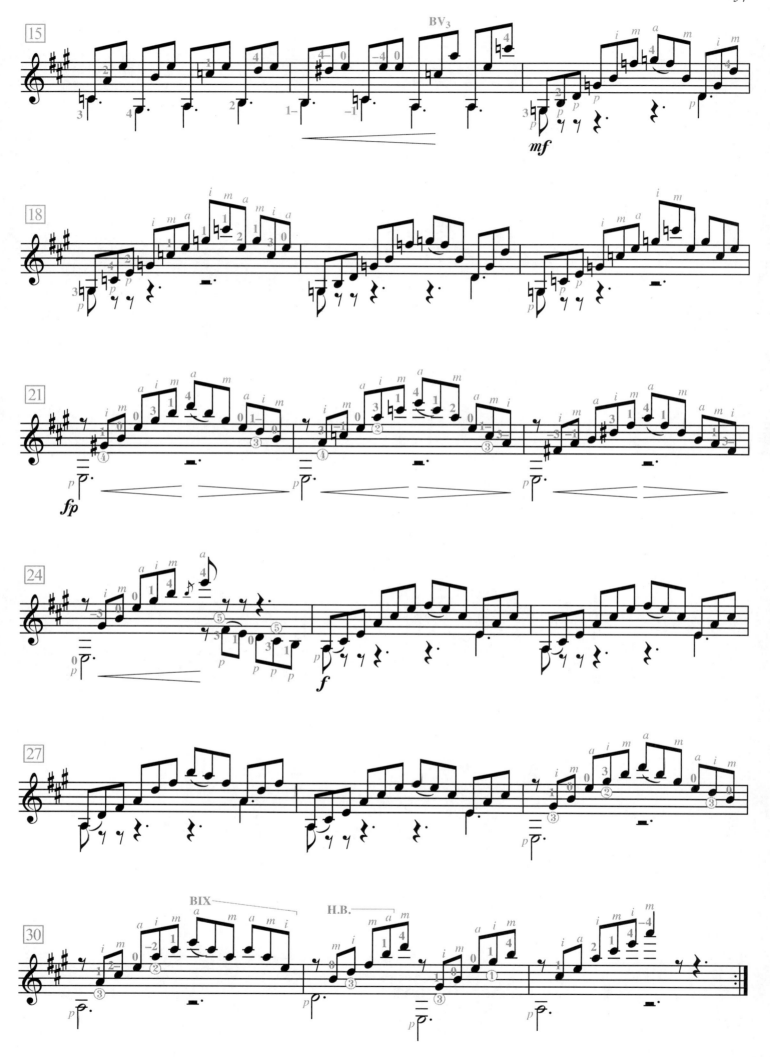

Etude No. 21

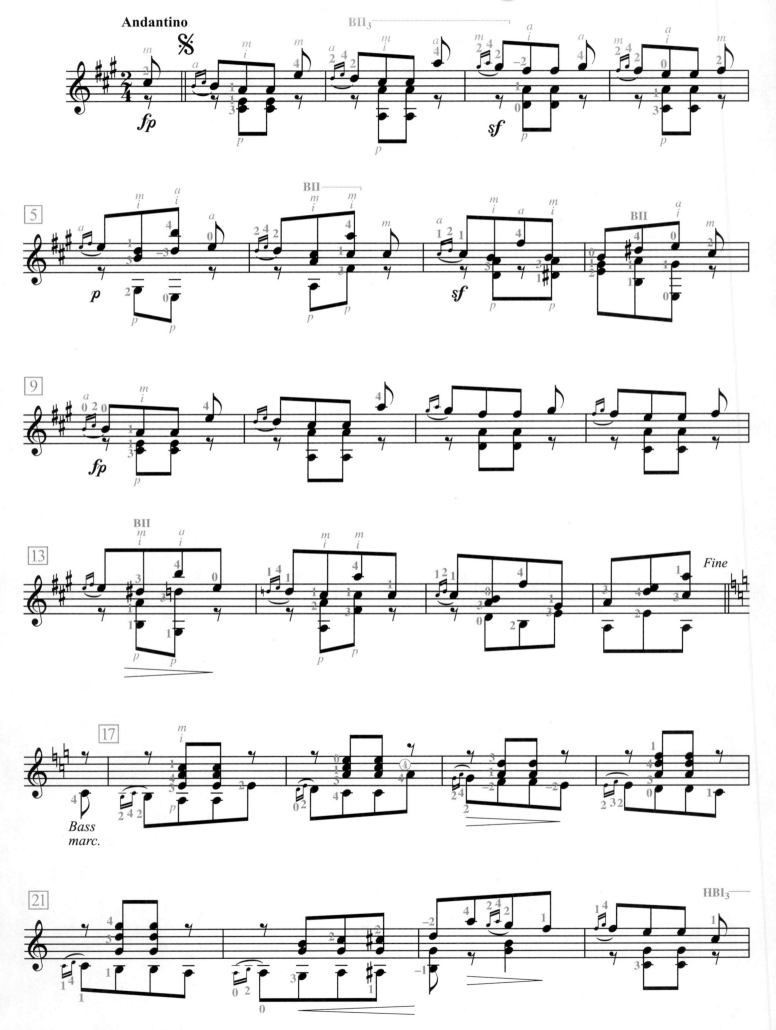

Etude No. 22

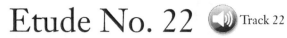

Track 22

Allegretto

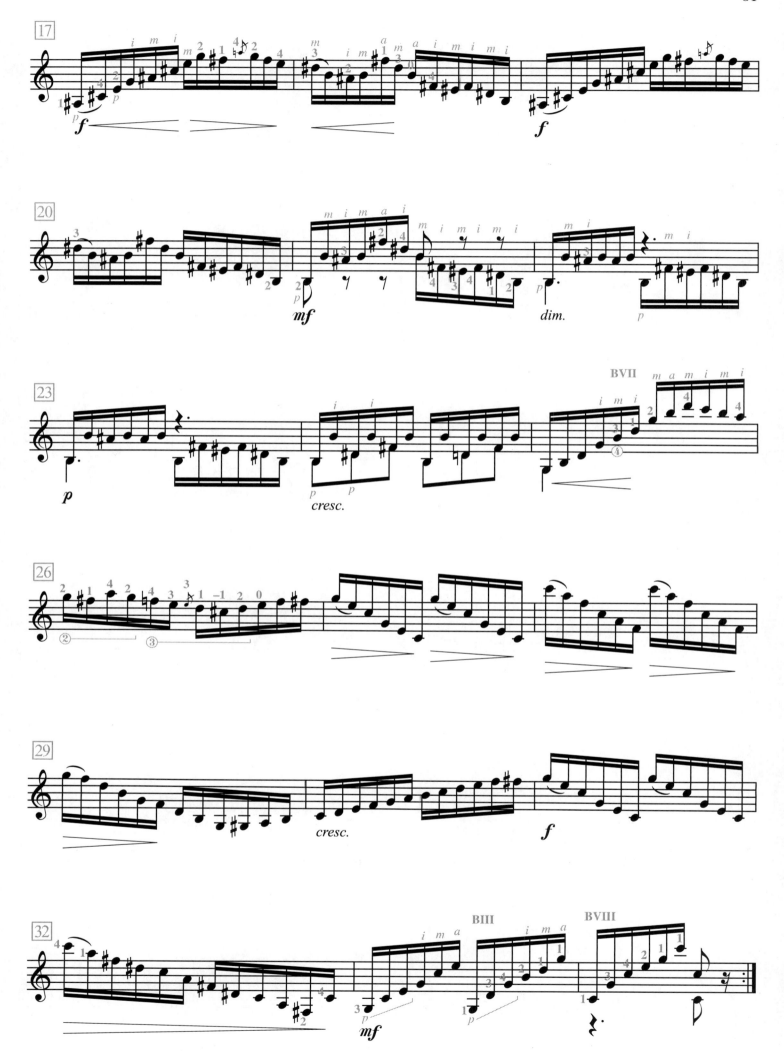

Etude No. 23

Track 23

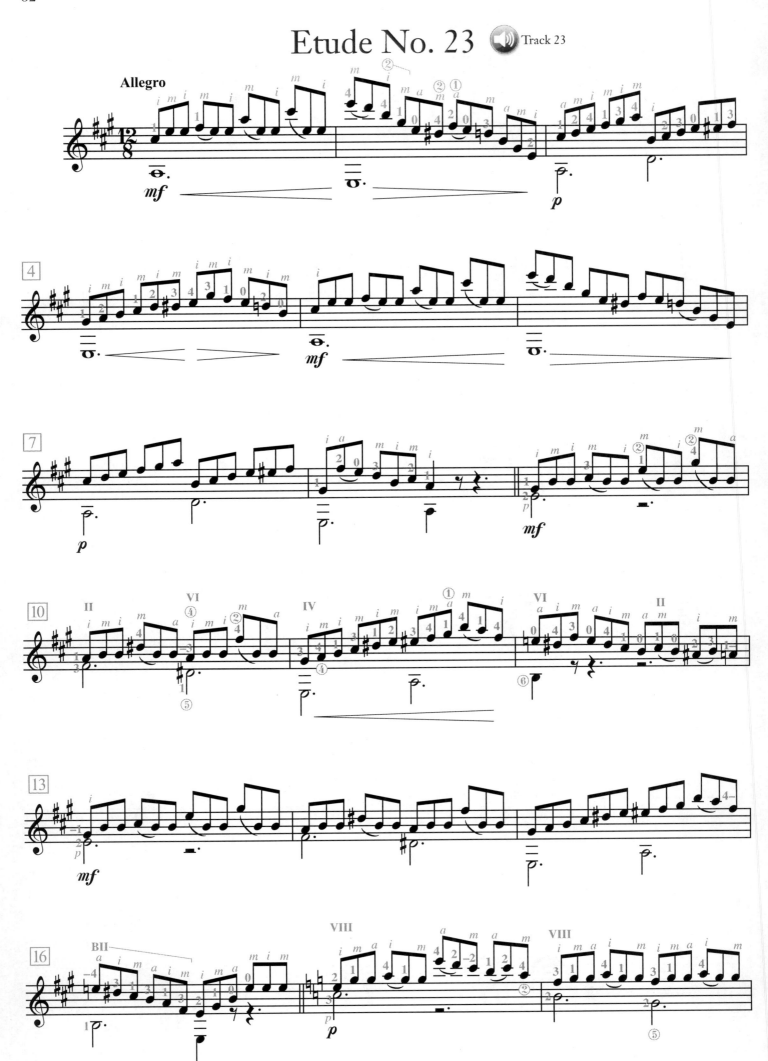

Etude No. 24  Track 24

66

This page intentionally left blank by the publisher.

68

Etude No. 25 Track 25